Metamorphosis

A Journey of the Soul

Ruth Soltman

Disclaimer

This book details the author's personal experiences. The author is not a healthcare provider. This book is not intended to diagnose, treat, cure, or prevent any illness or disease. Statements in this book are not intended as a substitute for medical advice. If you are having health issues, you should consult your medical professional.

Copyright ©2020 Ruth Soltman
All Rights Reserved

Angelworks Publishing
P.O. Box 747
Porter, TX 77365

ISBN 978-1-7358995-0-3 ebook
ISBN 978-1-7358995-1-0 Paperback

www.ruthsoltman.com

If you enjoyed this book, please take a few minutes to leave me a review. Thank you.

This book is dedicated to all those brave souls that came here now to assist humanity in this Great Awakening...I Honor You.

*The power you have inside of you can change lives,
yours and others. ~ Ruth Soltman*

CONTENTS

THE AWAKENING.................................1

CHANGE..................................25

RELATIONSHIPS 35

FORGIVENESS 49

LOSS.....................................59

SELF-CARE 87

LIVING AN AUTHENTIC LIFE 10203

ENERGY AND VIBRATION.................119

MAKING THE CONNECTION 12829

THE JOURNEY CONTINUES...............137

AFTERWORD 141

ABOUT THE AUTHOR 14647

Preface

This is the story of my own personal spiritual journey. My journey has taken me, and continues to take me, to places where I had not previously imagined myself.

This book has been written over many years. From the beginning I have been guided by Spirit to write about my experiences. As I have been reading back over the words I have written, one thing is clear, I have grown immensely since I wrote my first few words. I have grown in every way. My life has changed so much over the years and it continues to do so.

You must ask questions, research, look inside yourself and find *your* truth. My truth is true for me not for anyone else.

You cannot compare your experiences to those of anyone else. The spiritual journey is unique to each of us. Keep an open and receptive mind. You must be willing to question *everything*! Everything you have been told. Everything you *think* you know.

The answers you seek are already inside of you. You already possess the knowledge. You just have to remember what you already know.

This is my journey.

As I sit here ready to write, I ask for Divine Inspiration and Guidance. I ask that whatever words come to me, that they are exactly what someone needs to hear. I ask that you be blessed and inspired by these words. Words are enormously powerful. They can be healing and inspiring. Words can lead people to make positive changes in their lives. I ask for all the above. And so, it is.

Ruth Soltman

September 1, 2020

Acknowledgements

I would like to thank all the amazing people in my life and those that I have encountered along the way. Every person and situation taught me a lesson in life. I am grateful for every single one.

To my children:
My daughter Amanda who taught me perseverance.
My son Thomas who taught me patience.
My daughter Kristen who taught me compassion.
My son Josh who taught me to question *everything*.

To my parents Thomas and Judith for their unconditional love and teaching me some of life's greatest lessons.

Thank you to my Guides and Angels for helping me to find my path in this life, especially Archangel Michael for his constant love and protection, Archangel Gabriel for his guidance and inspiration to write, and Archangel Raphael for showing me how to heal.

Thank you for loving me and supporting me on my journey.

And a special thank you to Neale Donald Walsch for listening to his inner guidance and writing Conversations with God Book 1…the book that changed my life forever.

The Awakening

What is this "awakening" that everyone is talking about? What are you awakening from? What are you awakening into? What do you need to do? How do you get there? Awakening is a process you go through by which you *wake up* to the realization and truth of who you really are. You are Love. You are Light. You are Source Energy. You are all a part of the Oneness of life, forever interconnected with all forms of life.

When you begin to realize this, everything changes. Everything around you is more beautiful. The trees and grass are greener, the sky is bluer, the flowers are more colorful. You see beauty and love in the face of every fellow human being. Slowly you begin to shed your ego self. You work through life issues and past life issues to come to a place of complete unconditional love.

The process of awakening is a journey, a journey to remembering yourself. It occurs in many stages and comes only when you are ready. If you try to rush it or force it to happen it causes you to resist the revelations it shows you. When you are ready, it will begin. It will continue, always changing you, raising your vibration and continually awakening you.

When you first begin this journey, you have all this *realization* and newfound *education*. You just want to share it with *everyone*!!! Soon you conclude that people are not ready to hear it, until they are ready to hear it. Remember that you were in that place at one time, until you woke up. If you are not at a place within yourself where you are ready, there is nothing anyone can say or do that will make you ready. You awaken in your own time.

The process of awakening is not just a spiritual journey. It is a complete metamorphosis of the self- spiritually, emotionally, mentally and physically. Everything is broken down and rebuilt from the ground up. It strips away the layers of the ego self, a place of living from the mind and leads you to living from the heart and soul. What you are left with, what is revealed is your Spiritual or Higher Self...your Authentic Self.

This amazing process of awakening is not about learning anything new. It is more a process of seeing what has always been present. You were not able to bring it into focus before because your ego was in the way. As your ego begins to fall away and you live from a place of pure unconditional love, you see *everything* differently. You are a camera lens and as you turn that lens, more and more comes into focus and becomes clear. Everything that is in front of that camera lens has always been there. You just could not see it until you brought it into focus. With your ego in the way you could only see a partial picture. Now that the ego is retreating, everything is coming to you from the lens of Unconditional Love and Oneness. Life is no longer blurry. Everything begins to make sense. The difference is that now you are ready to understand it. It is almost feeling like you have been in a deep sleep and one day you just wake up. Everything in your world has changed.

It is amazing how you can make perfect choices and perfect decisions when those choices and decisions are coming from a place of unconditional love and not from the mind or ego. Once you learn how to do that, amazing things happen in your life.

Everything in your life will change, *nothing* will be the same as it was before. *You* will never be the same as you were before. That is the good news!

Your relationships will change. Your circle of friends will change. You will no longer be drawn to the people and situations that you were drawn to previously. You may have a sense of grief for these changing relationships, and that is okay. You tend to grieve when you feel loss. Acknowledge and honor whatever those feelings may be. It is okay to feel saddened. It is okay to feel loss. It is okay to feel abandoned. Those feelings are all part of the process and a major part of your spiritual growth.

There have been many people in my life that were important to me. People that meant so much to me that I could never even imagine my life without them. They were people that were in my life on a daily basis and people I thought were a huge emotional support for me. During this growth process I began to see the truth of these people. Sadly, I began to feel myself being drawn in a different direction, further and further away from them, until I no longer felt the need to communicate with them at all.

What I have learned from this is that some people have their own agenda. They are not looking out for what is for your highest good. This creates a lot of negativity. Every ounce of my being reacts badly to negative sensations. This is what caused me to gravitate towards people and situations that were of a higher vibration, people whose energy was more in line with my own. The loss of any relationship in life can be very disheartening, no matter the reason.

Some people live their lives from a place of complete ego. Now that you are rapidly changing and gravitating away from your ego self, you will find that you see things in a whole new light. People and situations that you accepted before, you will no longer be able to have in your life. They will feel it too. They will gravitate away from you as well. It is all a necessary part of the growth process and it is okay.

Do not ever feel that your feelings are *wrong*. They are what they are, and you do not have to apologize for them. Everything in your life is changing. People are leaving, situations are evolving. All these things must move *out* of your life in order for the new people and situations to move *into* your life. Everything is exactly the way it is supposed to be. You must trust that. Everything in your life, every person you have known, every experience you have had has been preparing you for the place you are right now and it is preparing you to become the person you are meant to be.

The awakening process is not a pretty one. It is a breaking down of your old self and way of life and opening up to new ones. It feels like your world is crumbling down around you. It feels like everything is coming to an end. It feels like it *is* the end and, in a way it is. Your old paradigms are falling apart, and new ideas and beliefs are emerging. You are peeling away the layers to get to the core.

This process shifts your thinking. This process shifts your perspective. You come to realize that the ideas and beliefs that you grew up with are not necessarily your own. Some were handed down to you from your parents and some were given to you by society. Sometimes you just follow along without even questioning. Other times you do question and you start to feel there is more to it than what you currently know. Search for your own answers to questions that puzzle you. Really think deeply and analyze your thoughts. Get to the core of why you believe something. Use your inner guidance. It is there for a reason. When you tap into it and listen to it, it will never steer you wrong. It is there for guidance and to lead you to that which is only for your Highest Good. When something does not *feel* right there is a reason for it, because it is not right for you. Go with your gut. Your intuition is never wrong. You just have to learn to trust it. Then you begin searching.

Synchronistic Events

The concept of synchronicity has always amazed me. The way something can come about in such an innocent way and finish with a huge grand finale. Unbeknownst to me at the time but a synchronistic meeting of a total stranger in a local bookstore would be the one key event that began my searching and awakening.

It was the mid to late 1990's, I was in the New Age section rummaging through books about Earth-Based Religions. As I was searching through the shelves, I noticed this woman kept looking at me. After a few minutes she asked me about one of the books she was looking at. We started talking and realized we had so much in common. We were both at a crossroads in our lives. We were searching for something but what it was completely eluded both of us. We were desperately yearning for more. We stood in the bookstore and had a three-hour conversation covering our interests and such in New Age and Alternative Health. She recommended a book to me called Conversations with God by Neale Donald Walsch. I had not heard of it but after her description I knew I had to read it. I was intrigued. I intuitively knew it contained information that I needed to hear. I borrowed it from my local library and began to read it.

I read the book slowly and let the information sink in. As I read page after page, it felt as if it was information I already knew but had forgotten. It was like when you are watching a game show on television and they ask a trivia question. You immediately answer and you answer correctly. You know it is not a subject in which you are knowledgeable, but you knew the answer anyway. You must have heard it somewhere before. How else could you have known? That is exactly how I felt. It also seemed as I read that book that it was written specifically for me. I felt that the world I had always known, *my* world, was crashing down around me. Every single word resonated so deeply within me, in my soul, that I knew it was my truth. I knew nothing would ever be the same again.

Most of the words I read were contrary to what I

had believed all of my life, and this really ticked me off. I felt angry that no one taught me the truth. I felt I had been lied to, manipulated and cheated. It took me awhile to process all these feelings. I realized that I had inherited the beliefs of my parents and that was not their fault. These were their beliefs and there is nothing wrong with that. I was realizing that their beliefs were not mine. Breaking away from the beliefs and ideals that I was raised with was not an easy task. Feelings of guilt, feelings that I was doing the wrong thing, feelings that my parents would not understand. These all flooded my mind. As I began to grow and figure out *my* truth and what resonated in my being, those negative feelings began to dissipate. We each have our own path to travel. We have to figure out what our truth is so that we can live in that truth each and every day.

In a sense I felt that everything that I had been taught my whole entire life was a lie or misconception. At the same time, I was relieved to know that there was someone else in this world that felt the same way I did. It was a moment of true personal empowerment. I felt as if I was beginning to see my true self. I was unveiling me to myself. It was a very spiritual experience.

It helped me to realize some truths. It is okay to believe differently than your parents. It is okay to believe differently than your upbringing. Although I was raised in a strict Catholic household, it never quite rang true for me. I believe all religious paths lead to the Light. They just take different routes to get there. And you can still find the Light *without* religion. It is all about what you feel a connection with and what resonates in your soul.

When you are able to peel away the layers of others' beliefs and form your own beliefs, you will be living in Your Truth. No one on this earth can know that for you. Only you can do that. You will know what resonates with your Soul when you hear it.

You will know what resonates with your Soul when you feel it. You will know your Truth.

As each thing was revealed to me from the book, I took much time to think about it and see how that truth *felt* to me. I realized that everything I had ever been taught was someone else's truth, not mine. The world as I knew it ceased to exist. And so, my awakening began, in search of the truth. *My* Truth.

What is Going On?

Flash forward about fifteen years, 2010 to be exact, a series of events unfolded in my life that took me in a downward spiral. I had just moved to a new city, lost my job, and was not having any luck finding another one. I could not understand how this was happening. I was guided and led by spirit to make this major move in my life. Why was it not working out for me?

I started getting down, almost to the point of being depressed. I was having headaches, stomach issues, dizziness and brain fog. I was exhausted *all* the time. I had no interest in anything anymore. And the uncontrollable emotions, oh my goodness! I was crying all the time, about anything and everything. I felt like I was losing my mind. I did not know anyone that was going through the things I was going through.

My intuition guided me to look up information about spiritual awakening. All the information I found described exactly what I was going through. I was so relieved to know I was not going out of my mind! If you are experiencing any unusual symptoms, I recommend you seek medical advice.

I did not know it at the time, but these symptoms were caused from the old, heavy energies exiting my body and new, lighter ones coming in. My body was adjusting to the higher vibrations.

Then the dreams started. They came every night, all night long. I was sleeping terribly, and I woke up sweating and exhausted every morning. I would talk, mumble, moan in pain and even cry during my sleep but, I did not make any sense. I would like to say that I learned a lot from these dreams but that is not the case at all. I rarely remembered anything at all. Sometimes I would wake up in the middle of the night and remember one just after it happened. Usually by the time I woke up in the morning, the memory of the dream was totally gone. As they continued, I would remember little bits and pieces. These dreams were manifesting from negative energy and emotions left behind from previous lifetimes. It was a comforting thought that once all this negative energy was released, my dreams would cease.

The dreams were very active and that was evidenced by my tossing and turning all night, waking up multiple times, and my finger-in-the-electrical-socket hairdo that I woke up with each morning.

One thing I do remember about these dreams, and I remember it with clarity, is that I was an active participant in them. I was there, living out whatever was going on in my dream. It was almost as if it was happening at the time and I was living it in the present. They were so powerful. That is one thing that made these dreams vastly different for me. The dreams I would usually have, it was like I was watching a video of myself but, in *these* dreams, I could see everything unfolding through *my* eyes, not the eyes of a lens. This made the dreams that much more real for me. For the longest time I thought it would be great to remember those dreams. Then I realized that if those dreams were so intense that they brought me to tears, it was probably best I did not recall them in the morning.

Dark Night

There comes a time in your journey where everything becomes dark, cloudy and murky. It is like you know the Light is there somewhere, but you cannot even begin to see it. Some call this The Dark Night of the Soul. I believe it is the shattering of the ego. It is when your Spirit Self takes over, stands up in the forefront and brings you back to who you are.

Just as love and fear cannot occupy the same space, your ego self and your spiritual self cannot be in control at the same time. In order for your Higher Self to occupy the forefront of your life, your ego must be diminished. You move from a place of fear and greed to a place of love, Unconditional Love.

While you are in this process, it is like you are at an in-between place. You are not completely asleep, but you are not completely awake either. It can last for a night for some or much longer for others.

For me, it lasted a long time, possibly years. I can equate this experience to a caterpillar's experience in a cocoon. The caterpillar begins making his cocoon. He is in a dark, quiet place. Everything about him and the life he knows is changing. He is literally turning himself inside out. He is breaking down, his very existence turning into goo. At this point in time he does not even recognize himself. He is getting ready to make a great transformation. This is what it felt like for me. It was a time of deep emotional work and healing on all levels. It was very dramatic. It was very intense. It was very overwhelming.

I could feel everything about me and my world was changing. I felt all these unresolved issues of my life coming to the surface all at once. I felt issues from other lifetimes coming up to be healed. Old relationships, pain, heartbreak, you name it, it was showing up. Situations that I had completely forgotten about reared their ugly heads. Situations I thought I had healed years ago but apparently, I had not. Each of these things can be overwhelming on their own. Here I was with *all* of them resurfacing at the same time! With all this raw emotion, the pain was unreal. It took a few days or weeks but once I stopped crying and got myself together a bit, I realized that all this stuff, this baggage, was coming to the surface for a reason. It all needed to be healed. This is when the hard work began.

I took one thing at a time, working through each situation. I figured out what I could have done better, figured out what went wrong and why. I thought about why things had happened as they did. *Everything happens for a reason.* I believe this with every ounce of my being. I live every day by these words, and I have probably said them thousands of times.

As I began to resolve my issues, I could see those situations with love. I could see those situations from the other person's perspective, not just my own. I was able to look at it as if I were a spectator watching a television program. You can see things much more objectively from that angle. This greatly helped me to heal the anger, disappointment, and everything that was holding me back. I could see the situations for what they were, Life Lessons. No more, no less. It was not all the hurt and drama that

I felt it was when I was living through it. Reliving it was entirely different. I did feel the hurt and such, but I could feel my way through it, and I came out the other side. I could see it on every level rather than only how it looked to me when it happened. I also realized that it was not all about me. When things happen in your life you tend to think that they are happening *to* you when, in fact, they are happening *for* you. Ask yourself...What is this teaching me? What is the Life Lesson for me to learn? Changing your perspective will help you change your feelings about the situation.

My awakening was accelerated at times. Spirit had been grooming me for years. In no way did I feel prepared for the changes I would go through. I may not have felt prepared, but my Higher Self knew the truth. It was time and I was ready for the transformation.

Just as I got to feeling comfortable in this new transformation, another one was preparing to birth from within me. The shift in my energy was palpable. Something deep inside of me changed. Something very deep inside of me was healed. I was holding on to things in my life that did not work. I was holding on to people that did not have my best interests at heart, and I was holding on to all the what ifs.

As I released these things, I felt a heaviness lift from me. It was as if my world was cloudy and full of thunderstorms and now, in the blink of an eye, the clouds had cleared, and the magnificent sun was shining on me. I had a sense of calmness and peace. I was a few steps further away from the control of my ego and a few steps closer to my soul. I felt an enormous amount of unconditional love for myself. I had a knowingness that my heart was completely healed. It was healed from all the pain I had been carrying around with me. It was healed from the heavy load I had placed on it. I felt so different. I felt free, energetic and *alive*! I felt complete freedom from the constraints that I had put on myself. I felt freedom from the pressure I had put on myself. I felt freedom from attachments to unhealthy situations. Free to live *my* life the way I wanted to live it. I was free to be me.

I have had many experiences like these over and over again for years. Each time I can feel the energy inside me changing and building. I can feel it working through me. I can feel a sense of heaviness just before another amazing breakthrough. Then there is this sense of knowingness. A sense of calmness and peace. Every single time I have some amazing new revelation about myself and my life. This is the path of my journey.

I am beginning to see that we do not experience this *Metamorphosis* only once in our lifetime. We grow and evolve and *morph* many times over the course of our lives. We are continuously changing and shedding our old ways. Different circumstances, different experiences, all cause us to shed our negative skin and bloom into a more spiritual being.

One thing I have realized for sure, no matter how much you *think* you have healed a past issue in your life, it if is not completely healed, it will keep showing up until it *is* healed. It may show up in different areas or forms, but the situation will incite the same feelings and emotions that you felt from the unresolved issue. I sometimes think the Universe exposes you to certain situations similar to ones you have experienced in the past simply to show you how far you have come and how much you have changed. When you are faced with a situation that causes you great pain, similar to one you have had in the past, and your reaction to that situation is completely different than it was in the past, you are able to see how much you have grown and changed.

Just like the butterfly cannot go back into the chrysalis and become a caterpillar again, I will never be the same person I was before my transformation. I have become that which I was born to become...my Authentic Self.

When you acknowledge and step into the person that you were born to be, your true authentic self, it is *the* most empowering feeling you will ever have.

All the pain and releasing that this process takes you through, these are labor pains. In the end, what you give birth to will be far more amazing than anything you could have imagined. Go through the process. Be conscious of the process. Respect the process. Be kind to yourself as well. You are giving birth to a new you.

Change

Change is doing something differently than the way you have been doing it. Many people fear change. It is taking a leap into unknown territory and yes, that can be a little daunting. You do not want to do anything different, yet you want specific outcomes that you are not getting by doing what you are doing. Change is inevitable. Change is what keeps you from stagnating. If it were not for change, you would never move forward in life. There would have been no invention of the car, television, or computer for that matter. Change always happens whether you want it to or not. You can accept change, or you can fight it all the way. In the end, it always wins. The process would be much easier if you could just *go with the flow* instead of always trying to swim upstream.

Most fish go with the flow of the stream. That is the easy route. Going against the current is tough. Even the strong ones do not always survive. Life can be difficult enough without going against the current. Accept change. Embrace it. You do not have to like it or even approve of it. Just accept it and let it be. It is going to happen regardless of whether *you* give it permission to, or not. So, make yourself more comfortable and a bit happier, just let change happen! There is not a whole lot you can do to stop it anyway.

I knew I wanted to make some changes in my life. I wanted to be that which I always felt inside that I could and would become. Change is never easy. In fact, many people do whatever they can to avoid it. There are a seldom few who welcome change. I am one of those few. I thrive on change. Why would you want everything to always stay the same? That makes for a stagnant environment. Whether you realize it or not change does happen, with or without your blessing. It is up to you to accept it and go with the flow or to resist it. You only make yourself miserable when you resist change. You just have to adjust your perspective and learn to *see* it differently. Change is a new opportunity for growth.

Change rarely happens overnight. It is not like you go to sleep one night as a caterpillar and wake up the next morning as a magnificent butterfly. It is usually a slow process of numerous minor changes that all coincide to create major changes in your life. It gets you all stirred up inside. You can feel something is about to happen. You just cannot pinpoint exactly what it is.

Life is full of changes and decisions. Decisions that you make create changes in your world and have a ripple effect that expands outward. The decision to take a new job, move across the country or even follow a dream will create changes that you cannot even fathom. Many new things will occur. New people will come into or go out of your life. You will have new experiences that will create more change. Every choice you make creates a change in circumstances. Everything happens for a reason and everything happens the way it is supposed to.

When I was younger, I never liked for anyone to get too close to me. I felt that if they *really* knew me, they would not like me. Not sure where that thinking came from. I never pretended to be someone I was not, I just did not offer a lot of myself into conversations. I am not talking about random people that I would meet. I am talking about everyone-classmates, co-workers and even family members. I did not realize it at first, but I think that was something I had done all my life.

Adults called me shy. Later in life I learned that I was an introvert. Then it all made sense. When I was a child, I was a bit of a loner. There were no children in the neighborhood for me to play with so I just kind of kept to myself. Before I knew it, I had created a shell around me, and I let very few people inside. I realized that this is not who I wanted to be. I cracked that shell and little by little I have let people inside. At first it was very difficult and painful to let anyone get that close. However, with the addition of each new person that I let in, it got easier and easier. Now the shell is completely gone, and I recognize myself, the person I have become, for the person that I always wanted to be.

Writing this book is just another part in my healing process. It is difficult to share myself with others in this way. I feel wide open and vulnerable. I am exposing the deepest parts of my soul. This is what I used to avoid doing. This has been a spiritual growing and healing for me. I am putting myself out there, warts and all, for the entire world to see. This is me. The *real* me. This is who I am and who I was always meant to be. You may like me, or you may not. That is none of my business. What matters most is how I feel about myself. I like me. I love me. I am proud of myself and this magnificent journey I am walking. That is *my* choice.

It took me a long time to get to a place with myself where I was comfortable with that. If someone likes you or they do not, it does not matter. The important thing is how *you* feel about yourself. When you reach this place and no longer care what other people think of you, you will feel absolute freedom. It is very empowering.

The only person in the world that you can change is yourself. No matter how hard you try, you cannot change anyone else. That is up to them. That is their journey. You can assist others and you can offer information or guidance, but you cannot force someone to change. What you can do is offer your love and support. It took me a long time to understand that. Once I did, everything fell into perspective and I am a much happier, content person.

Hearing it and knowing it are two totally different things. To hear it you must have the physical ability to hear. To know it, you must have the mental and spiritual ability to see it inside of yourself. This is not an easy task, especially for people who have trust issues. I struggled with this for years. I have had many issues with trusting myself. It was one thing to know it, but it was another thing to *know* it. I always felt it but had a difficult time trusting what I felt. It was a long process, but I finally listen to that inner voice. If I did not, I would not be writing this book. It seems the more I write the more release and relief I feel. By the time I finish this book I will have lost 20 or 30 pounds of excess emotional baggage!

Emotional baggage is such a comical term. You all have it. It comes from living life, having relationships and experiencing love. It starts in your childhood and you carry it with you wherever you go. You get to a point in life where the load is too heavy to carry anymore and you must let it go. It may not be easy, but it is necessary for your own emotional well-being. Every experience you have ever had is recorded in your cell memory. Although things may appear to be gone from the surface, many times the baggage is buried much deeper and it takes a shovel and a pick to dig it out. Once you do, and you get rid of it, you can lead a much happier life.

There were a lot of emotions from the past that I thought I had dealt with and they began to resurface. I had to work through them again and again until I was finally able to let them go.

I really needed to heal and purge myself of all this excess baggage that I had been carrying around with me and I did not even know it! Afterwards I felt so much relief. Although the memories of those experiences will remain with me always, the pain associated with those memories is just a thing of the past. You really can heal those old wounds and recover from all that pain. The journey was a real learning experience for me. I learned a lot about myself.

When you really want to make a change in your life, whatever it may be, devise a plan. Do it in stages. Then you can make the changes gradually rather than all at once. Of course, life throws changes at you all the time. The easiest way to deal with those is to go with the flow.

I have always felt very blessed that just the *right* people were put on my path at just the *right* times in my life. What I never stopped to think about was that the universe put *me* in someone's path as well. Always at just the right time. Everyone comes into your life for a reason. Sometimes we are the teacher and sometimes we are the student. We can learn something from everyone.

Many things happen during your lifetime. Changes are constantly occurring. Some changes such as marriage, a baby or new job opportunity are welcomed. Others such as divorce, illness or the loss of a loved one are much dreaded. One thing is for sure, change is inevitable. You can either accept it or you can fight it all the way. The choice is yours.

Relationships

Relationships of any kind may be the most challenging thing you face in your lifetime. Whether is it a parent-child relationship, siblings, friends or a romantic relationship, these may present you with many challenges and changes. People that you are close to often challenge you in many ways. They may challenge your belief systems. This can be an incredibly positive thing if you can keep an open mind. It is great to hear new perspectives on what you believe. It may help you to realize your beliefs are not what you thought they were, or it can help you to cement those beliefs on an even deeper level within yourself. They may challenge you to move beyond your comfort zone or they may hinder your progress. You need to be planted firmly in who you are so that you cannot easily be led astray from your path.

Parents and Children

The parent-child relationship can be an interesting one. Some people spend their entire adult years trying to recover from their childhood and the poor relationship they had with a parent. I was so very blessed to have had wonderful parents. They were far from perfect, but I had a great relationship with both of them. I am also very blessed to have an open and honest relationship with each of my children. There is so much love that I can feel my heart chakra swell just at the thought of them.

As parents you need to be cautious of the words that you use with your children. Children are *very* literal. They hear what you *say*, not what you *mean*. Sometimes what seems like a little thing to a parent can be something life changing to a child. A small negative comment could change the way a child views themselves forever. It is crucial to a child's well-being to hear positive words of love and praise. It is crucial to a child for them to have a positive view of themselves.

It is of paramount importance that you *listen* to your children. They are very wise, and very psychic. They do not know fear, it is taught to them. It is important that you listen, believe, and support them in all they say or do. It is ironic how as children you are taught to conform in school, at home, and in public. You are taught to do things the way others want you to do them. These are the children, like me, who grow up trying to please everyone except themselves. You teach your children to live *inside the box*. When they grow up, they struggle for many years trying to reteach themselves to live *outside of the box*. Why not teach them as children that there is no box? Teach them to be themselves. We basically all want the same things-to be loved and to be accepted for who we are. Why not teach your children this from the beginning? Then maybe they would grow up to be happy, healthy, adjusted individuals. They *are* individuals after all. They are not alike. Why try to group them that way? Why try to label them? Let them be themselves. They are unique. They each have their own unique path to walk. Celebrate their uniqueness. Celebrate their differences. Show them that these are the things that make them special.

Where does the disconnect come in? Where on the journey does a child go from feeling good about themselves to feeling bad about themselves? This happens even when they are growing up in a positive, loving home.

The teen years can be very trying for the teen and the parents. They are constantly changing and growing on every level. Their bodies are rapidly changing. They are beginning to think differently than they did as a child. They are beginning to see life through a different lens. Sometimes that lens is tainted by negativity and fake people and sometimes it is soaked in positivity and authenticity. They begin to form their own ideas and beliefs about the world based on their experiences. They make new friends that share their ideals. This is a time of enormous growth. It is so important to do and say things that empower your teen. Words and actions to make them feel good about themselves. They need to know they are loved and accepted for who they are. Be kind. They are just discovering all of this for themselves and it can be a scary place sometimes. If they feel accepted and loved now, they will grow into young adults feeling the same way. They will not look outside of themselves for validation of who they are. They will innately know who they are. Let them make decisions even if their choices do not turn out for the best. Every experience contains a lesson they can learn. Help your teen to see that. With that perspective they will have every confidence in making decisions. With a little practice they will be making the best decisions for themselves and their lives. After all your job as a parent is not to rule their every move and force them to be what you want them to be. Your job as a parent is to raise a human being that is a kind, loving, positive, functioning member of society.

Siblings

Sibling relationships can be very touchy. They can be very close-knit or there can be a lot of rivalry. Sometimes children, or even adults, feel they are not being treated equally or fairly by their parents in comparison to a sibling. Sometimes they may feel a sibling is loved by their parents more than *they* are. Siblings are either fighting with each other or for each other.

Friendship

Friend relationships can be the most amazing relationships. From a young age you believe that your family likes you or loves you because they are your family. You feel that they *must*. It is when we start to make friends that we feel we begin to engage with people who like us just because. They do not have to, they choose to. This can be a very empowering feeling as you are growing up. Just one more reason to be yourself. Shed the ideas that other people put on you of who you are. Make that discovery and determination on your own. You do not want friends that know you with your mask, with the fake person you present to the world. You want friends that know the real you. For that to happen, *you* must know the real you. It is never too early in life to make those discoveries. Find out what makes you tick. Find out what your likes and dislikes are. Stand up for who you are. You are Light. You are Love. You are Worthy and Magnificent.

Romance

Some people completely lose themselves in a romantic relationship. They lose sight of who they are and what they want in life. I know what that is like because I have done that. You focus all your attention on the other person and *their* needs and wants and you ignore your own. You may feel that you are being selfless, but this situation does not benefit anyone. You lose yourself, your identity. You lose sight of what you want, what you like and what you need. You live your life for this other person. Relationships like that will eventually fall apart.

When you are broken and in pieces you have nothing to give to another person except for a piece of yourself. When you are whole you have everything to offer. You must be a whole and complete person before you can contribute to a healthy relationship. People look to someone else to make them happy and to complete them. That does not happen. Happiness is an inside job. It is something you must do for yourself. Only you can make you happy. Happiness is a choice. We have to make it every day.

The best relationships require communication, trust, love, and authenticity. When you live your life from a place of authenticity, you live from a place of realness. You know who you are, what you want, and you do not hide yourself behind a mask. You are you. You are the person that is left after all the layers of who others wanted you to be are gone. You are whole. You love yourself unconditionally. You connect with another person on every level - physical, emotional, mental and spiritual. You have mutual love and respect for each other. You share in each other's triumphs and tribulations. You are each other's rock.

Being in a romantic relationship can be extremely rewarding. It is nice to have someone to come home to. It is nice to have someone ask about your day. It is nice to have someone to lean on when your load gets heavy and burdensome. Those are not reason enough to get into a serious relationship. Many times, people get together for the wrong reason. You may be feeling lonely or bored in life. You may be feeling old or unattractive. Then someone comes along and says exactly the *right* thing to make you feel better. You are not on a time schedule. There is no hurry. Take your time. It will happen when it is meant to happen. The Universe will send you your perfect person when you are ready. Not when you *think* you are ready but when you are *truly* ready.

When you terminate a romantic relationship, spend some time to heal before you decide to move on to another relationship. You need time to heal from the pain and get to know yourself again. You are going from being part of a *couple* to being an *individual* again. I know, I know, you were still an individual when you were part of your relationship too. What I mean by that is that when you were part of a couple you did things together, activities, sports, etc. with your significant other. It is time to experiment and find out what *you* like to do when not influenced by someone else. Maybe there is a hobby or activity you always wanted to try but your significant other was not supportive. Now is the time. Take the time for yourself. Honor yourself in that way. Time has passed since you got into that last relationship. Chances are rather good that you have grown and changed since that time. Get to know yourself again. Learn to love yourself again, unconditionally. When you rush quickly into another relationship, you do yourself a great disservice. That is unfair to you and the person you are getting involved with. Discover yourself all over again. Enjoy spending time *with yourself.* Spend time in nature to rejuvenate your Spirit. Spend time in meditation to calm and relax you. Spend time with your family and friends that support you. Laugh, be joyous, and heal.

Yourself

There are so many types of relationships that can come into your life. The very most important relationship that you will *ever* have is the relationship with yourself.

Love yourself first. That is not prideful or selfish. If you cannot learn to love yourself how can you love anyone else? How can you give something to someone that you do not possess yourself? If your cup is empty you cannot share it with anyone. You have to fill your own cup. You have to make yourself whole. You have to peel away the layers of who you *should* be that were put upon you by others. You have to do the work. You have to dig deep within yourself. You will always find the answers there. Remember to be kind to yourself. Treat yourself the way you would treat someone else. Say kind things. Do kind things. Your body hears everything you say and will react accordingly. Only speak to yourself and about yourself in a kind, loving manner.

If you do the work, you will have a clear understanding of who you are and what you want. Never settle for less. You deserve the best. You are worth it.

As you learn more Universal Truths, unravel more layers and further advance your soul's journey, look back on some of the major relationships and heartaches you have had in your life. You can see things now that you could not see before. It helps you to put things in a new perspective. You can see why things happened the way they did. You can see each situation as an experience to grow and to learn more about yourself. Being able to see past events more clearly, seeing the *why* of things that have occurred in your life, helps you to grow even more. It is fine to temporarily visit the past and to heal past hurts and relationships. You cannot get stuck there. You must live in the present.

Forgiveness

You have often heard that forgiveness is something that you do for yourself, not for the other person. Although that is true, it is not always an easy thing to do. How do you forgive someone who has hurt you?

It is important for your personal and spiritual growth that you move beyond the pain and hurt that can sometimes hold you back or keep you stuck in the past. When you release the pain, anger and disappointment, you relinquish the hold that those feelings have on you. Then you can move forward.

Nothing can affect you or hold power over you unless you allow it to. With that being said, it is sometimes difficult not to feel that you are affected by angry words or someone hurting your feelings, whether it was intentional or not. Your ego or mind self tells you that you should feel bad, that those are the appropriate feelings. If you begin to see things from more of a higher vibrational space, a spiritual place, instead of from that lower vibration of your ego mind, you will begin to see things from a much different perspective.

When someone judges you, says harsh words to you or hurts you in some way, it has *nothing* to do with *you!* They are reacting that way due to the place they are at in *their* life. These are usually feelings that they have about themselves that they project onto someone else. A lot of the time it is the person or persons they feel closest to or most comfortable with that they lash out at.

Every experience that you have is an opportunity for you to learn and grow. You may not have control over the things that happen in your life, but you do have control over how you react to them. When you have *expectations* and others do not live up to your expectations then you experience disappointment on a *human* level. You must move beyond that to experience life from more of a spiritual place. When you do, you experience life with unconditional love and you no longer come from a place of expectations.

Forgiveness has been a huge part of my personal journey. I have never had a difficult time forgiving someone when they were truly sorry. It can be much more difficult to forgive someone who does not feel any remorse for what they have done or someone who has not been willing to apologize. For me, the most difficult person to forgive in my life was me. I am not sure why this is, but we seem to be so hard on ourselves about everything.

Forgiveness is a gift and it is a gift you give to yourself. You release yourself from the anger and anxiety of holding on to situations that no longer serve you. They are a burden and only persist in weighing you down. When you choose to forgive you are not saying that the hurt or issue did not happen. All you are saying is that it no longer causes you pain and you can move on.

When you can remember and relive the situation in your mind without all the pain that caused it, you have released the hold it has on you. You have healed.

Part of my waking up required me to bring up old situations in my lifetime and past lifetimes and heal them. This required a tremendous amount of forgiveness. I was sitting there one day trying to figure out how to do this since many of these people were no longer in my life

While doing this major spiritual work, I felt an enormous need to look back over my life, my relationships and people that I felt had *failed* me.

People that had hurt me or taken me for granted, even if they did not realize they had done so.

Forgiveness Exercise

Here are the steps that I took to acknowledge and release those issues that were still affecting me and holding me back in my life. This remarkably simple exercise worked to heal me from the pain of past hurt and it worked amazingly well. It will help you to heal your hurt and your heart too.

Examine your life and your relationships, past and present. Acknowledge those that you feel caused you any harm or pain. Look at situations you did not heal from or have closure with. Include every situation that ever caused you pain that you have not resolved. Everything from the high school bully to the significant other that broke your heart. Remember to include yourself as well. Think of the times you have let yourself down or done things to disappoint yourself. Remember the times that you may have intentionally done something to hurt someone. Remember *all* those things.

There will be certain memories that will stand out to you. Trust that they are coming up to be healed. Yes, I know, this may take awhile. It may be hours, days or months. It depends on which issues come up for you, which issues you have not yet healed. The process is simple. You could work on one issue a day or a week. Take your time. That is okay. It will take as long as it takes. Do not rush through the process. Give yourself time. Be patient with yourself.

Write a letter to each person coming from your place of ego or mind. Express your anger and disappointment in the way you felt you were treated. Get mad! Yell at them! Tell them what they did and how it made you feel! You will feel a lot of emotion arise out of this exercise. It may take you a few minutes, a few hours, days or weeks to complete each one. That is perfectly fine. It will happen as it needs to and as you are ready. You have many years of relationships and events to remember and work through. It is important to remember *all* the relationships that you feel caused you unresolved pain and anxiety. You are still hanging on to that pain and even if it has been suppressed, it is the cause of your issues today. You need to clear all of it out so you can fill that space inside of you with unconditional love for yourself. Then you will be able to move on.

Once the letters are written you are ready to complete the exercise.

Read each letter aloud, one at a time. Yell! Scream! Cry! Get out all the painful feelings you feel. You are coming from a place of ego mind confronting this pain, but you will be forgiving and releasing it from a place of Spirit or your Higher Self. Once it is released, you will feel much lighter and these things that once caused you a great deal of pain will be a mere memory. They will no longer affect you and you will be free to move forward in your life.

After you have read the letters aloud, read the following with their name inserted:

(Person's name) You have hurt me in this lifetime or past lifetime. You have left a crack in my heart with your actions. I choose to move on and let these things go. I choose to heal my heart and move on.

(Person's name) I will no longer let the pain you caused me in the past cause me pain in the present. I release this pain, anger and hurt. I heal my heart and I move forward.

(Person's name) I know that the things you did that hurt me were about *you* and not about me. I forgive you and wish you the best life has to offer.

I release it and I let it go!!!

When you acknowledge and release all of this you release it from a place of ego mind since that is where it took place. When you forgive and let it go, you do it from a place of unconditional love. You empty that place of hurt deep inside of you and fill it up with unconditional love. Then the healing *really* begins. You will feel lighter and more joyous. You may even begin to remember things that had been buried or covered up by your pain. Happier memories will begin emerging surrounding these people and situations in your life. The most amazing thing for me was that the current issues in my life that had been caused by not dealing with my past issues, they began to fade.

This seems like a very simple exercise and it is. It can be time consuming so if you need to do it a little at a time, that is okay. Just do it.

The healing that took place in my life from these exercises was immeasurable. It will be a very deep, profound experience for you as well. Just keep an open mind, an open heart and set your intentions. I hope you will accept this challenge, examine your past experiences and heal them into the future.

Loss

Losing someone that you love it is a sad fact of life. You lose some people thorough divorce, some through your own growth and some that leave this world for another. Their beautiful Spirit leaves their earthly body and they transition. I have lost so many people in my life. Three of them were the greatest losses of my life...my grandmother, my dad and my mom. From each of these losses came tremendous insights and lessons.

My Grandmother

My grandmother, Ruby, was the sweetest and nicest woman. Everyone that knew her, loved her.

Although she had only one child in this life (my mom), she had enough love for a dozen children. My grandma was a highly active person. She did everything from cooking and cleaning to home repairs and lawn maintenance. She was an amazing woman. When I was young, I loved to go and spend the night at her house. My grandpa was an over the road truck driver, so he was gone most of the time. I would wake up to bacon and home-made pancakes! She was the absolute *best* cook and baker. I loved making homemade cinnamon rolls with her!!! It was so much fun!

She was a firm believer in God and the Bible. We had many great conversations and no matter what I asked her, she would always tell me the truth.

Out of all my grandparents, I was the closest with her and remained that way as I grew into an adult. My oldest daughter's first Thanksgiving was at my grandmother's house. She had her first taste of mashed potatoes there. My grandmother adored her first great grandchild. Sadly, that was the only one she would know.

I do not remember the exact year that she was diagnosed with breast cancer, but I believe it was in the fall of 1984 or 1985. It was a huge blow to our family. She was the first one in our family to become terminally ill. I was in my early 20's and my siblings were younger.

I remember being at the hospital when she had her biopsy and they ended up doing a mastectomy. She did not know that would be the outcome of her surgery until she woke up. I remember thinking to myself how awful it would be to wake up and get that kind of devastating news. The news only worsened. It had metastasized and she needed chemotherapy and radiation. Her body did not react well to the treatment and she kept declining. My mom went out to her house to care for her. She eventually went into Hospice Care, sometimes at home and sometimes at a Hospice Respite Center.

The morning of May 2, 1986 my dad called into work. It was very unusual as this was something he did not do unless he was extremely ill. He also kept my brother and sister home from school that day. He said he just had a feeling he needed to stay home. My mom called him that morning and said my grandmother was not doing well at all and they felt she did not have much time. They all headed to the Hospice Center to see her. She had siblings that were there from out of town too. She was surrounded by love. I was living in a different state at the time and I could not be there. Shortly after they all arrived, my grandmother transitioned. I found out via a phone call from my mom. I was devastated. I was so upset that I was not there and that I did not get to say goodbye to her. I was able to make it for her funeral though.

For many years I carried around a ton of guilt that I was the only one in my family that was not there. Guilt that I did not get to say goodbye to this woman that meant so much to me. I tortured myself for years. One of the most profound lessons I would learn in my life was born from this experience. *Everything happens for a reason.* I do not always know the reason but that is not what is important. This lesson has carried me through some of the toughest times in my life. I still believe this with all of my being.

My Father

As a child growing up, I thought my parents were amazing. They seemed to know everything, and they seemed to always be right. That is a child's way of thinking. Children idolize their parents. They see them as these all-knowing gods. As I grew up, I realized that my parents were only human. I did still think they were amazing but of course they did not know everything, and they were not always right. They had not changed. My perspective had changed.

My father was a great man. He was a hardworking, kind, compassionate man. He instilled many valuable things in me. Things like honesty, integrity, loyalty, respect for myself and others, and a high moral compass. He taught me to tell the truth, love and accept others unconditionally and treat others the way I wanted to be treated.

He gave me a place called *home* and that was not always in the physical sense of the word. I knew he was *always* there for me, no matter what.

The way he lived his life, he was a great example to others. He had a great personality, and everyone liked him. He always did for others. He would literally give someone the shirt off his back. He believed that everyone was equal, that no one was greater than or less than anyone else.

The greatest gift he gave me was the gift of assisting him with his transition. This was a process that spanned a little over three months. We found out in March of 2005 that he had lung cancer. He had a Pancoast Tumor and it was entwined with nerves and blood vessels that made it inoperable. He was not told at the time, but he had Stage 4 Cancer. My family was devastated by this news. My dad was the greatest. He was everybody's hero. He had so much love for his family. The little things meant everything to him. Some of his favorites were playing video games with his grandkids, eating a cheeseburger, and he had a great love of golf which he handed down to my youngest son. His grandkids called him Papa and he was the kind of grandpa that would lay down on the floor and play with the kids knowing it would take him 15 minutes to get back up again. He was always so proud of his family. They were everything to him.

After he was diagnosed, I moved in with my parents to take care of him and help my mom out. She was also caring for my elderly grandfather who was suffering from Alzheimer's Disease and Dementia. It was during this time that my mom was diagnosed with Colon Cancer and had to have a portion of her colon removed as well. Fortunately, they were able to remove the cancer with surgery alone. It was a challenging time for everyone.

It took the doctors a while to get my dad's pain under control. That may be an exaggeration. I am not sure it was ever *under control,* but they got it to a place where it was somewhat manageable for him.

I am blessed to have been there with him during the last months of his life. I was blessed to see the shift in his perceptions. He was no longer worried if the electrical bill was paid or if there were groceries that needed to be bought. His only concern, and I mean *only* concern was spending time with those that he loved. Many people came by to see him. He enjoyed those visits immensely.

He would repeatedly tell me that he was not going to make it until Christmas. It was summertime and he was always a worry wart, so I think his statements were dismissed at first. He became persistent with these claims. There was not a doubt in his mind that when December 25th came around, he would not be here on this earth. Christmas was our family's favorite time of the year. It was always a big deal. My mom and dad especially loved to spoil their grandkids at this time of the year. So, my dad decided since he was not going to make it until Christmas, he wanted us to have Christmas in July. He wanted one more Christmas with his grandkids. So that is what we did. He insisted on shopping for his grandkids. He wanted to pick out all their gifts. He talked me into taking him shopping. We had to stop every little while so he could rest a bit, but he did it all. He got everything he wanted to get. We wrapped the presents. We put the Christmas tree up and decorated it. We made turkey and stuffing and all the foods we usually had on Christmas Eve. The grandkids all opened their gifts. I do not know who was more excited, the kids or my dad! We had a magnificent celebration! It was beautiful! It felt very fulfilling that we could all honor his Last Wish. I know he was grateful for that day. He knew all along that he would not make it until Christmas. He was right.

My dad and I had many great conversations. One has always stuck with me. He told me that my mom was an extraordinarily strong woman. He said she was the strongest woman he has ever known. He made me promise him that I would get her out of the house and encourage her to do things after he was gone. She was the love of his life and he was of hers. He did not want her to drown in her grief. He wanted her to live and to be happy again. He completely underestimated her stubbornness. Trying to get my mom to do something she did not want to do was like trying to get blood from a turnip.

He tried traditional treatments, but his condition continued to worsen. The cancer was spreading into his spine and into his brain. He had to face his greatest fear, being paralyzed, as a tumor on his spine continued to grow. He became paralyzed from the waist down and needed assistance to do most things. He was devastated by this. My dad was the one who always did for others. It was difficult for him to let others help him. He had to surrender to that now. It was his time to let others care for *him*.

He was sleeping most of the time now, slowly slipping from this world into the next and back again. We witnessed him "playing cards" with his grandpa and eating an ice cream cone with him as well. His grandpa was one of his favorite people. He passed when my dad was young. I am sure his grandpa was there to welcome him to the other side.

After my dad got sick, he said he wanted to *go* with just my mom in the room, holding his hand. He did not want a lot of people around. People were there around the clock for weeks. The night before he passed the house was full. My sister and I slept in his room in case he needed anything throughout the night. When morning came, she had to leave for a bit to take care of her family. My dad's breathing was getting a bit shallow. I went in to check on him and see if he needed anything. He grabbed my arm in a panic and said "Ruth, help me, I think I'm dying". It broke my heart. We knew he was dying and there was nothing I could do to help him at this point. I could only love him and support him. Even though it has been over fifteen years since that August morning, I remember it like it was yesterday. I felt so hopeless, so powerless, so helpless. I did what I could to make him comfortable. My mom came in to sit with him while I took a much-needed shower. When I came out of the shower I passed by his room. My mom was still sitting there, holding his hand and keeping him company. He looked different as I entered the room. My mom said he was breathing very slowly. She was waiting for him to take another breath. He never did. He was gone. It was totally heartbreaking and beautiful at the same time. He went exactly the way he wanted to, with my mom holding his hand. I was devastated that he was gone but I felt such joy for him. Joy that he was no longer suffering the intense pain that he had been suffering. Joy that he was released from the confines of his earthly body that was so badly broken. Joy that his Spirit was free and that he was reunited with loved ones he had lost throughout his lifetime.

After my dad passed, I saw how extraordinarily strong my mother really was. We all thought that she would grieve herself to death, that she would just stay in bed and sleep for months. She did not. She got up every single day, got dressed, and continued to live. She lived almost twelve years without him. I was so proud of her. Losing the love of her life, the man she had been with for over forty years, completely broke her. She was so devastated by her loss. She missed him and grieved for him until she took her last breath. I can only imagine the joy, love and celebration when they were reunited on the other side. The love we have for others never dies.

I learned so much from my father and I am forever

grateful this man was my father and raised me to be a good, honest person. The greatest lesson I learned from him is *the importance of quality time with your family.*

My Mother

After my dad passed, I stayed with my mom for few years as she was adjusting to life without him. Many years later, she moved to Texas where me and my daughters lived. She bought a house near my daughter and I moved in with her. She had always had many health issues and as she was getting older, they were increasing. She could not do it by herself anymore. She needed help.

I did everything for her that she could not do for herself. As time went on, there was less and less she could do for herself.

She had been having headaches or something and we went to see a neurologist. They scheduled tests and we went in for the results. Not sure how but somehow when they did her scans, they got part of her lung in the scan and it showed a mass in one of her lungs. She went in for a biopsy.

In May of 2015 she was diagnosed with lung cancer. She had the same type of tumor that my dad had. We went to see an oncologist. My mom had seen how much my grandmother and my father suffered as a result of traditional treatments, so she declined surgery, chemotherapy and radiation. With all of her health issues she did not feel she was a good candidate for surgery anyway.

She continued to live her life as she had, and I continued to care for her. In the early months of 2017, she became much more tired than usual. She was going to bed earlier, getting up later and napping during the day.

She woke up on a Sunday morning in March and called for me. Little did I know this would be the beginning of the end. I ran into her room. She said she thought she was having a heart attack and to call 911. The paramedics arrived very quickly and tended to her immediately. They confirmed it was not a heart attack and they took her to the hospital. I followed in my car and was there when they arrived. They discovered that one of her lungs had collapsed. That was the reason it was so difficult for her to breath and she felt the heaviness in her chest. They recommended she go into Hospice Care.

The hospital bed arrived, and we rearranged her bedroom. I slept in a twin bed next to the hospital bed in case she needed me during the night. We laid there every night talking about life, the sunrises, and anything that she wanted to talk about. She told me how much she loved me and how much she appreciated everything I did for her. We held hands every night as she was drifting off to sleep.

She had been under Hospice Care for about a week or so and on a Wednesday morning she woke up acting very off. Something just did not look right. I called the Hospice nurse and she came right out. My mom had suffered a stroke. It left one side of her body damaged. Her left eye and the left side of her mouth were droopy. It was difficult for her to say what she wanted to say. She was no longer able to get out of bed because she had lost the use of her left leg. It would not move and would drag behind her. Hospice said she would probably not make it through the weekend. She would not want to live life this way. Out of state family members were contacted.

She was in and out of it the next morning. Family members were on their way. Hospice arrived. They said she was getting close to leaving. We knew it was getting close. You could tell. Everything felt different. The Hospice Chaplain was there and he began reading from one of her favorite books. As she heard the words, she was letting go. The more he read, the faster and faster she was declining. I wanted to yell "Stop, don't go" but I did not. We were gathered around her, holding her hands and telling her how much we loved her, and we would be ok. You could feel and see this strange sensation going on inside of her. Something like a trembling, a vibration, something. The only way I can put it into words, and words cannot do it justice, is this-it felt like a freight train running inside her. The momentum was that powerful. It started out slowly then full speed ahead! It was almost as if you could see it and you could certainly feel it. I knew that train was coming for her and that it was going to take her away. Then she threw herself back on the bed and her eyes rolled back in her head. You could visibly see a wave move over her body, beginning at the top of her head. As it moved from the top of her head, through her body, to the bottom of her feet, her complexion turned to a grayish hue. Then in an instant, it was all over. She was gone. It was the most heart breaking and awe-inspiring experience of my life.

As I watched my mother take her last breaths, I was flooded with so many different feelings and emotion

Enormous sadness flooded my soul. My heart was shattered into a million pieces. I felt a sense of joy and relief that her pain and suffering were over. I felt so alone even though the house was full of people. I felt this enormous wave of energy soar through my center as her spirit left her body. It was an experience I could not put into words, until now.

The room was full of tears. Even though we knew for a couple of years that she was terminal nothing prepares you for the loss of your mother. Nothing. Maybe it is because hers was the first heartbeat I ever heard. Maybe it is the bond from growing inside of her body. I do not know. What I do know is that the loss is monumental.

She had lived 74 years in the body that had always worked against her. She had illnesses that started in her childhood. To some degree she was a prisoner in her own body. She needed to be set free. She was ready to fly! She shed her earthly skin and soared into the Heavens. It was her time to go home. She was ready. We were not.

I remember sitting outside later that day crying and thinking to myself...OMG I am an orphan! I realize how silly that sounds, especially since I was 53 years old at the time. That is how I felt in that moment-abandoned, alone and isolated. I was now the Matriarch of my Family.

Going to the funeral home and the days following the funeral are much of a blur. Actually, the first six or eight months after she passed are mostly a blur. My grief was immeasurable. I was just moving through the day, drowning in my grief. I was not living at all. If there was something I *had* to do I did it, otherwise you could find me laying on the couch, with the television on, until it was time to go to bed. I do not really remember what I watched, I was just kind of numb and out of touch. My life had been turned upside down. My center, my purpose was gone in an instant. I had to figure out who I was without her.

It has been a little more than three years and I still grieve a little every single day. I miss her more than ever. I do not think that will ever subside. I do know that she is with my dad and other loved ones. She is waiting on the other side for the rest of her family to come home. She will be there to greet us all and rejoice in our arrivals just as her parents and husband were there to greet her. What a reunion that must have been.

We had many deep, meaningful conversations sitting outside with our coffee on the patio. Three of them really stick out in my mind. One morning, out of the blue, my mom apologizes for being a burden to me. I told her I never felt like she was a burden and that I genuinely enjoyed everything I did for her. She said she knows how difficult it is to care for someone 24/7 and if I ever feel overwhelmed or do not want to do it anymore, I should let her know.

I told her that would never happen. She carried me in her body for nine months, raised me and took care of me when I could not take care of myself. I told her that I considered it an honor and a privilege to care for her and to spend the last years of her life with her. We both hugged and cried.

A second conversation was when we were talking about her death. She told me that it would be extremely hard on me and that nothing in life prepares you for the loss of your mother. She said that I *can* live without her and I will. I told her that I know that I just do not *want* to. She said she wished she had felt that way when her mother passed. She said she honestly did not think she could live without her mother.

The third conversation that sticks out to me was when she had started to decline. She said "Ruth, I always thought I would have more time". We were so blessed to know almost two years prior that she was terminally ill. It gave her and everyone else time to say goodbye, time to say things that needed to be said and time to do things that needed to be done. Not everyone gets that time. It was truly a blessing.

She wanted me to post on Facebook for her. Here is what I wrote:

> Nearly two years ago I was diagnosed with Lung Cancer. I opted out of conventional treatments and my quality of life has been pretty stable since. About a week and a half ago I began a decline and am now receiving Hospice Care at home. I was blessed to spend 44 years with the love of my life. I raised three wonderful children. I have been able to see all six of my grandchildren grow up and become amazing adults. I have also been blessed with six great-grandchildren and number seven will be arriving this year. I have had a very good life filled with so much love. I am grateful for every minute of every day.

Please send me lots of love and positive energy. I love everyone so much and will miss you all!!!

Less than 24 hours later, she made her transition.

My mom taught me many things in life but, most of all, she taught me love, Unconditional Love. I will be forever grateful and indebted to her for that. My life has so much more meaning because she was here. I think the greatest lesson that I learned from this experience was that *Time is Precious. Appreciate every moment and enjoy the little things.*

Legacy

My parents may be gone from this earth but their legacy of love, and all the sparkles of Light that they left behind, will continue to light the way for others for generations to come.

When I am gone, I want to be remembered for how much I loved, without condition. I want to be remembered by how much I gave, how much I inspired people. I want to send a ripple of love out into the world that will be felt for many generations to come. This is the legacy I want to leave behind. Think about the legacy you would like to leave and plan accordingly.

Healing from Loss

How do you heal from loss? I believe it is different for everyone. Everyone heals differently. I do believe however, that you need to face the loss and deal with it, or you risk the chance of it tainting everything in your life for years to come. You cannot just push your feelings under the rug and hope that they will go away. They will not. You must go through it. As you go through it, you will grow through it and come out on the other side of it. Sometimes in your pain it is difficult to see but, look for the silver lining. Figure out what this experience is trying to teach you. Every significant experience teaches you a significant life lesson.

Loss is devastating, debilitating and painful. It can tear people apart and it can bring people back together. Take time to heal. Do not give yourself a time limit. It takes as long as it takes. It is different for everyone. Take all the time you need. Be angry. Grieve. Work through your pain and come out the other side of it. Ceasing to grieve does not take away any love that you had for the person you lost. It just means that you have accepted the loss and you are willing and able to move forward with your life.

How do you know when you have healed from such a huge loss in your life? I believe it is when you can think of that person and smile. You think of them and only warm, fond, happy memories come to mind. It feels like the pain of losing them is a mere glimmer in the background.

For a long time is was too painful for me to look at old photos so I avoided doing that. Since I have healed the pain of those losses, I can now look at old photos and smile. I have enough memories of my departed loved ones to keep me warm for this lifetime. I know how blessed I am. I have had and still have so many loving people in my life. I am so very grateful.

Loss has been a great teacher to me. Loss has taught me not to take people or time for granted. Do not just assume if someone is in your life today that they will be there tomorrow. Do not put anything off until tomorrow that you can do today. Your tomorrow may never come. Appreciate what you have and who you have in your life.

After three years of grieving the most monumental loss of my life, I am finally getting back on track and moving forward with my life. I have decided to take my mom's words to heart. We do not know how much time we have on this Earth. I am no longer putting anything off. I am living in the moment. This is not to say that I do not set long term goals or make plans ahead of time. I do. Some things take time to come to fruition. I just do not take time for granted anymore. I no longer *assume* I can do it later instead of sooner. This changing of my thoughts and my perspective have had a huge impact on my life. Living in the moment takes away the grief and sadness of living in the past and the anxiety and stress of living in the future. There is only now. That is all we truly have.

Message that friend you have been too *busy* to call. Tell that someone how much you love them. Spend time with the people who matter the most. Live so that if you lost someone you loved tomorrow, you know that it was clear to them how much they meant to you, without a doubt. Do not leave anything unsaid. Leave a legacy of love long after you are gone from this world. That will give all those you left behind the courage, strength and love to move forward.

Self-Care

What is self-care? Seems like an obvious question. It is taking care of yourself. What does that mean? How do you do that? Self-care requires care on all levels- physical, emotional, mental, and spiritual. It is fulfilling yourself and doing what is best for yourself on every level of yourself. Do not confuse self-care with self-ish. There is nothing selfish about taking care of yourself.

Self-care is something that is crucial to each of us, yet it is something that was never talked about when I was young. Like many others, I was raised to believe that you always put others before yourself, that their needs and wants come first. If you put yourself first, you are selfish and self-centered.

Growing up with these beliefs for so many years made it more difficult to change my thought patterns, take better care of myself and put myself first. My spiritual growth taught me that I needed to take care of myself first. If I was not happy, healthy, balanced and centered and my cup was not full I would not be able to give of myself to others. While I understood this on one level, it took me a long while to comprehend it on all levels and make changes in my life. It has only been the last few years that I have implemented these changes. I no longer say *yes* when I mean *no*. I am no longer a *people pleaser*. I no longer do things just because someone asks me to or wants me to. I do them if *I* want to. This has been a much healthier way of life for me and it can be for you too.

Self-Care on every level is a necessity. It is crucial to your growth and evolution. You need to be healthy physically, emotionally, mentally and spiritually.

Physical Care

The physical aspect is obvious-eat healthy, drink a lot of water and exercise.

While there are many external environmental influences that you cannot control, you need to do your best to avoid these or counter them with positive reinforcements. You cannot avoid things like pollution, but you can physically detox yourself and avoid things like chemically filled food and water sources. You are the only one that can decide if you feel these things need to be avoided in your life. Like everything else, it is a personal choice. Your Higher Self knows and will relay that information to you in one way or another. Know your body. Listen to your body. It will tell you what you need.

Emotional Care

Emotional Care requires you to be in control of yourself, from your feelings to your behavior. You need to detox yourself from toxic people and toxic relationships. This may be a real challenge as those toxic people are sometimes people that are closest to you.

What is a toxic relationship? It is a relationship or situation in which the behavior of your partner is poisonous or damaging to you. For example, a relationship that is dominated by control whether physical or emotional. Toxic relationships suck the energy and life right out of you. Eventually as you change yourself to try and please your partner, you completely lose sight of who you are. You lose sight of your value and your worth.

When you engage in toxic relationships the toxicity and negativity have very detrimental effects on your health. They can affect every avenue of your well-being. It can affect you physically, emotionally, mentally or spiritually. The ripple effect can extend to *all* of these areas. Stress alone can have many negative effects on your physicality. Just imagine the damage that can be done from a toxic relationship.

You may love them and feel that you can *fix* them, you cannot. There is nothing *you* can do to fix anyone else or *make* them change. Only they can do that. If you are in an abusive relationship, I urge you to get the help you need to get out of that situation.

You can love people from a distance and not engage in their toxic lifestyles. Your health is much more important than their drama.

Mental Care

Mental care deals with your psychological wellness. This requires stress relief and relaxation. Stress has a terribly negative effect on your physical body. It can cause headaches, suppress your immune system and cause even more serious problems if it continues for a long period of time. De-stressing yourself is a necessity. It is vital to your overall well-being.

You need to declutter your mind and be conscious of how you fill it. Everything you perceive through your physical senses affects your well-being. This includes movies, music, television and even conversations.

Meditation can be a great tool to assist you with clearing your mind and living in the moment. You can find meditations with music, sounds, or even Guided Meditations that take you on a beautiful journey inside yourself. You will know what feels right. Your physical body will react. You just need to listen. You need to balance every aspect of yourself and your life.

Spiritual Care

Spiritual health deals with our belief systems, our

values and morals. In order to figure things out for yourself, you must go within for that is where the answers lie.

Spiritual health is crucial to your growth as a human being. It is here that you find your true self. It is in your spiritual self that you uncover and form your beliefs. It is here that you find unconditional love for yourself and others. It is your spiritual self that shows you the way. Your intuition guides you, like a GPS, if you are tuned in and listening. Your intuition is the guidance of your Higher Self, your connection to Source. It is always correct and always knows what you need for your highest good. You just need to listen.

Find your connection to your Higher Power. You may connect outside in nature. You may seek out a church or religious program that fits with your beliefs. It can be powerful to surround yourself with like-minded people. A small circle of like-minded friends is a great support system for your spiritual self.

Be Happy

What makes you happy? I mean really, genuinely happy. Is it all the stuff your money can buy for you? Is it the people in your life? The people you love? Ask yourself this question...If you were to lose *everything* you have-your home, job, bank account, material possessions-would you continue to be happy? What about the loss of a loved one? Do you continue to live fully or feel guilty for continuing your life on this earth without them? Do you let those things and situations define you and your happiness?

Who is responsible for your happiness? Your significant other? Your parents? Your children? Of course not! *You* and *you* alone are responsible for your happiness. You have to *choose* to be happy. It is a choice you have to make each and every day.

Where is this happiness you have been striving for? It has been residing inside of you all along. You did not know because you did not look for it there. You can live your entire life and never come to this realization. It is all about being present and grateful for what you have. You look *out there* for happiness. You look to your job, money, possessions and other people. You do not realize that happiness is in each and every one of you. Some of you choose not to acknowledge it and you stay in your misery. You tell yourselves that you will be happy when _____ (you can fill in the blank). You are always looking for the next best thing. You tend to keep yourselves so busy *doing* things so that you do not have to think about it. You put on a show that you are happy and that everything is wonderful. But that is just a facade.

In order to be happy, you must live in the present. You cannot dwell on memories of the past and you cannot live in the anticipation of the future. You have to be fully present and grateful for all that you have right now. This moment is all you ever truly have. Think about it right now. This very moment is all there is. After five minutes, what is it? It is now. Half an hour later, it is now. Now is all there is.

Some people think that they would be happier somewhere else, in a different job, home, relationship etc. They are surprised to find that when they achieve those things their *happiness* is only temporary. Then they feel they would be *happier* in a different job, home, relationship etc. You go through life this way, living in the future, and never being genuinely happy. You are always looking for happiness outside of yourself and, of course you never find it. Your *happiness* issues are not out there in any of those things. Those issues reside within you. It is not until you isolate those issues and work on those issues, that you will be able to find true happiness. When you are genuinely happy, all those exterior things are just icing on the cake. Without them, you would still be the same happy person that you are.

There will always be situations in life that you have no control over. What you do have control over is how you react to those situations. Just like you, I have had many obstacles in my life. I have lost many people that I love. I have lost my worldly belongings a few times over, had less than a dollar in my bank account for many, many months, been jobless, even briefly homeless. Although they were difficult times it did not stop me from my inner peace and happiness. I always felt very blessed and felt as if I had more than I needed. That is not to say that I was not upset or grieving during these times. I surely was. The difference is that I processed my grief quickly and began to see the bigger picture. I began to see the lessons the Universe was trying to teach me.

You cannot be happy when you are trying to live up to someone else's expectations of who you are. You cannot be happy when you are living to impress others with your stuff. You cannot be happy when you do not love yourself unconditionally. You cannot be genuinely happy when you do not accept yourself for who you are.

No *thing* can make you happy. No *person* can make you happy. Many relationships fail due to people believing that your happiness can be created by someone else, that someone else is responsible for your happiness. If you believe that, it will be difficult for your relationship to succeed. Putting that kind of pressure on another human being, for them to be responsible for *your* happiness, who can live up to that? The truth is that *you* are responsible for your happiness. If you are not happy it is *your* responsibility to find out why. It is *your* responsibility to work out your issues. It is *your* responsibility to choose to be happy.

For this moment, choose to be happy. Find something that gives you joy. Think about that. Focus on that. Feel it. Hold the energy of that thought, that emotion. Keep your thoughts and energy positive. If you are not used to being in a state of happiness this may take some practice. Try positive affirmations. Tell yourself...I am happy and grateful for all that I have. Say it until you believe it. Practice, practice, practice. Soon you will be doing it without even thinking about it. It will become second nature. Positive change will raise your vibration and attract more positive things into your life.

Many times, we think that happiness is something outside of us. I would be happy if I got that new job, new house, or new relationship. The truth is that happiness is not *out there*... Happiness is inside. It is a choice you make every single day. The world around you can be falling down but you still maintain an inner peace. There is no one that can make you happy except for you. When you choose to be happy, it helps to alleviate stress. It raises your vibration. It helps keep you centered. It is good for your body, mind, and spirit.

Self-Love

Self-love is huge component of self-care. You may feel it is difficult to love yourself. After all you know *everything* about you. You know your thoughts, your fears and your deepest desires. You are aware of everything you have ever done or thought about doing. When you do things that you are not proud of you question yourself. How could anyone love me? How can I love me? It may not happen overnight, but you can learn to love yourself.

Daily affirmations can be extremely helpful on your journey to loving yourself. When you repeat the same words over and over you begin to believe them. Look in the mirror. Talk to yourself. Tell yourself how much you love you. Compliment yourself. Say positive things to yourself just as you would to someone else. Be proud of yourself. Be proud of your progress. Be kind to yourself. Treat yourself the way you want to be treated by others.

Tell yourself "I love you." Tell yourself "I am amazing." Self-talk, whether positive or negative, has a huge impact on your overall well-being. If you do this every day, after a few weeks, you will see a huge improvement.

Let me tell you something from my own experience. I have so much love in my heart. I love my family beyond words. I love unconditionally. As much as I loved everyone else, I did not fully love myself. I was never taught about self-love. My spiritual journey took me to this place. I learned how to love and appreciate myself for the magnificent being that I am. As I grew to love myself more and more, I could actually feel my heart chakra expanding. Once I began to fully love and accept myself for who I am the love I felt for others multiplied exponentially. I feel love on a much deeper level now, for others and for myself. When you encompass self-care as a daily routine, everything about yourself and your life will change. Your perspective, attitude and energy levels will change. You will become more balanced and centered.

Think of ways you can care for yourself. Do something special for yourself. Treat yourself. Buy that book you have been wanting to read. Go get that specialty coffee that you only have on rare occasions. Take a hot bubble bath and relax. You deserve it. You seriously do.

Living an Authentic Life

Authenticity is living in the truth of who you are. It is putting yourself out there and not hiding behind a mask of some kind. Authentic people are real and everything you say and do is true to who you really are. You are *always* your true, authentic self. No matter what.

Fake people pretend to be something they are not. Sometimes this is because you think it will impress others. Sometimes you are just not in touch with who you are. You are like chameleons; you change who you are according to your environment and the people you are with. This is because, for whatever reason, you have not discovered who you are. You do not know yourself at all. Therefore, you conform to whoever you are around. It is incredibly sad really that someone does not know who they are. That is an extremely dangerous place to be. You can be so easily influenced. You cannot be genuinely happy if you are living the life someone else wants for you. You have to know yourself and want it for yourself.

I have been on a journey of self-discovery most of my life. It is so interesting to continually learn new things about myself. Sometimes I even surprise myself! Every experience in my life has taught me something. Every experience has brought me closer to my true self.

How do you live in your authenticity? You open yourself to the truth of who you are and why you are here.

You are Light

You have a spark inside of you. You may call it Love, you may call it Light, you may call it God/Source. Call it whatever resonates with you and acknowledge that it is alive in each and every one of you. This Light is what makes you your beautiful, individual and unique self. Some of you choose to live in this place of Light, some are frightened of it while others ignore it altogether. Time and time again situations will arise in your life when you will move into that place where you were meant to be, and you will begin to shine your Light. When you live from this place of your Authentic Self, you let your Light shine and let others see your Light, *amazing* transformations take place.

These transformations have a ripple effect. Just as a stone thrown into a pond ripples through the entire pond, touching every droplet of water, when you shine your Light and live from your place of Light, it ripples out into the world. It touches the people around you, your city, your state, your country, your world, your entire Universe. We are ALL connected in that way. Eventually the energy that you put out there touches everyone. Make sure you make a positive ripple in the ocean of humanity.

Shed your fears and let your authentic self shine through. Become empowered and your life will never be the same. It is okay to be you! You are not a carbon copy of anyone. There is no one like you. You are beautiful and unique. That power you have inside of you can change lives, yours and others. Brighten your Love Light, allow your inner glow to reveal itself to the world. Shine your Light for all to see. Give your thoughts to that which are positive and good. You truly are…The Light of the World.

Purpose and Passion

What is your purpose? What are you passionate about? I believe your purpose and your passion are two different things. Your purpose is the reason you are here. It is the mission you signed up for before you came to earth. Your passion is your gift that, when you are using it and sharing it, it sets your soul on fire and fulfills your purpose. I believe your purpose and your passion are connected. You have been given your gifts (passion) as a means to fulfill your purpose.

You are here for a reason, something you came to this earth plane to accomplish.

Some people know their purpose early in life and they spend their entire life living in their purpose. Others learn their purpose much later. It does not matter *when* you discover why you are here. What *is* important is to acknowledge it and to live it. You may be a gifted musician or singer. You may be gifted with wisdom or compassion. You must discover your gifts. You must find out what sets your soul on fire. Then you figure out how you can live in that place and how you can best serve all of humanity. When the time is right, you will begin to remember. This is something you already know, your Higher Self knows. It is written on your soul. Over the course of your life, choices you make or situations you encounter, may cause you to lose sight of that purpose. It is always inside of you, sometimes it is buried deep but, it is always there.

When I was young, I always felt my purpose was to become a mom. After my four children were grown, I no longer felt I had a purpose. I just kind of wandered through life for awhile.

One day after I moved to Texas, a friend told me about this Psychic Buddhist Monk in Houston. People would come from all over to have a meeting with him and they would wait for hours. He made his services available to everyone. I had an opportunity to go and see him. I was told to write down any questions that I wanted to ask him and that he would answer them after he got done with the reading.

He took people back in groups of eight. We sat in a

small room with the group and he would call you in one by one. To my surprise he looked right at me first and motioned for me to come with him. We sat on the floor and he began to tell me many things about myself. He covered many years of my life and the information was correct. Then he looked me straight in the eyes and told me I needed to finish writing my book. I knew at that moment he was the real thing. I was the *only* person in the entire world that knew I had started writing a book. There was no way he could have known. I asked him what my life's purpose was and he told me it was *to heal humanity*. He told me that God wanted me to touch his people. I was completely overwhelmed by this so I did what anyone in my position would have done. I shut down and I looked the other way. I ignored his words and I did this for many years. I did it until I could not do it anymore. The pulling and nudging from the Universe was just too strong. I began to reflect and try and figure out what I was supposed to do, how I could live in my purpose.

Then it came to me. I could touch God's people with my thoughts, words and ideas.

What does it mean to *find your passion* and how do you do that? Your passion is that thing that sets your soul on fire and makes you come alive when you are doing it. Think back to when you were a child. What did you *love* to do? Was it drawing or painting? Learning? Helping others? What were the things that brought you pure joy when you were a child? It is not something someone else can tell you. It is something you *know* way down deep inside. It is the gifts you were born with. Only *you* can do what you do, the way you do it! When you open yourself up to the possibility, amazing things can happen. Sometimes life can overshadow that knowingness, but it is still there.

When you were a child, you did things out of pure joy. You did not do them because you felt you had to or because you felt you should. You did them because you *wanted* to. Children do not have those types of filters, but adults do. Many times, you do things for all the wrong reasons. You do them because you feel you should, you feel it is what you are supposed to do, or you feel it is what is expected.

For me to find my passion, I had to reexamine my life. I had to be honest with myself about all the things that brought me joy, things that interested me and things that made me feel good about myself. As you grow in life, you sometimes forget those things. You sometimes bury your desires so deeply that you do not even know they are still there anymore. Then something happens to reawaken them. Things reveal themselves to us when we are ready and not a minute sooner. This was the case for me as well.

I had forgotten that when I was a child, I had a great love of writing and I even remember starting a school newspaper when I was in grade school. I wrote poems, short stories and articles. Words can inspire you, uplift you and change your perspective. They have great power. Words backed with emotion can change a life. Words give meaning to things and to experiences. They can be shared to inspire others, to help heal and to change a life. Something triggered these memories in me, and Spirit began nudging me to write. Every time I write, my soul rejoices. I feel enormous joy, happiness and I feel fulfilled. Nothing else can compare

Once I remembered this, I found a website online that was looking for contributing writers. I contacted them immediately and sent them something I had written. Except for when I was in school, it was the first time anyone had read something I wrote. I was a little nervous, but I decided to step outside of my comfort zone. They loved my writing style and my writing. I was so excited! The first article I wrote was about forgiveness. I had more likes than I ever imagined I would. I got so overwhelmed with emotion when people would comment. They pointed out specific things that I said that really resonated with them.

My soul was overflowing with joy and gratitude. I knew this was what I was supposed to do.

Sometimes you let your ego get in the way of your *self*. You let yourself be conditioned through family members, life experiences and society into believing that you do not know what you want for yourself. How many people do you know that are genuinely happy, fulfilling their soul's desire and living a genuine, authentic life? How many people do you know that get up, day after day, go to work and come home, reliving the same basic experience every day without any sense of fulfillment? They are not living their purpose or their passion. They are not living in a place that is their authentic self.

When did this start? When did you stop listening to your inner voice that *knows* what you want to do? Somewhere along the way you stopped listening. You bought into the ideas of society and what you *should* do. You bought into the ideas of how your life *should* look, what things you *should* have. Some people stay in that place their entire lives. Others get to a place where you begin to *wake up* from the dream. You wake up to reality. You wake up to yourself.

Getting to this place is not an easy task, especially if you do not have a clue to who you are or what you want in life. It can be downright frightening to wake up and not even recognize yourself or your life anymore. You are not quite sure who you are or what you want but you know *this* is not it!

What do you do when you get to this place? You can ignore your wake-up call and go on with your life as it was, or you can find your passion and remember your purpose. The choice is yours. You can stay where you are, or you can grow and evolve.

Imagine what a different world you would live in if everyone was living in their purpose and living life with passion! And everyone can! You must remember what it is and find a way to live it!

I found a way to incorporate my passion for writing with my purpose of giving of myself and helping heal humanity...Writing words to inspire and help others.

You came to this earth with an intended purpose and the passion to live in that purpose. It is your obligation to remember and act on that information. The hard part is remembering exactly what that is. When you figure it out and you live *in* your purpose, *with* your passion, that is when you shine the brightest. That is when you are living in the place of your true, authentic self. No one can do what you do, exactly the way you do it and as well as you do it. Only you!

There are things you do with such a passion that it sparks a fire in our soul. You have specific gifts you brought with you to help you on your journey.

Many times, you do not even realize that what you have is a gift because it is how you have always been. Then one day you may meet someone that is not like you at all and then you become very aware of your gifts.

My passion is people and writing. Writing is the vehicle through which I can convey unconditional love, teach and inspire others and help people. When I write and I am *in the zone,* and the words flow out of me effortlessly. It is as if Spirit is whispering the words in my ear and typing the letters through my hands. It is amazing to go back and reread what I have written. It hits me at my core and sets my soul on fire over and over again!

It has been my experience that opportunities, events, even people, come into your life when you are ready to receive them. When you are truly on your *correct* path, living in your Truth, everything seems to fall into place.

When you are traveling on your correct path your purpose is slowly revealed to you. It is a simple remembering, knowing and acknowledging who you really are and why you are here. You have chosen to be here, in this place, at this time. You have come here for a Divine Purpose. When you are living in your purpose life is immeasurably rewarding in *every* way. You feel unlimited love, joy and happiness. You know there are no limitations to your being. The only limitations you will ever have are the limitations you put on yourself through your mind.

You are powerful beyond your wildest imagination. You are capable of anything and everything. You are Unconditional Love. When you come to this realization and you quiet the mind you achieve things that you *never* thought were possible. You are only limited by your thinking. Keep your mind wide open. Do not limit yourself. Everything is possible.

Energy and Vibration

Everything around you is energy and has a vibration. You are energy. You are whirling sparkles of love and light energy dressed in human form. You vibrate at a certain frequency. Your vibration can change at any time. Your lifestyle can raise or lower your vibratory energy. There are many factors that attribute to your vibration. The things you eat and drink affect your vibration. The way you see life affects your vibration. Do you have a positive attitude about life, or do you tend to be negative? Do you feel your life is full of abundance or do you feel you are lacking? You can change your vibration at any point in time.

Whatever frequency you are emitting, that is the frequency that the Universe will match. It will send you things equal to your vibration. When we live and vibrate in the energy of fear, the Universe will match that and send us more things to fear. Love has an extremely high vibration. When you live in a vibration of love you are sending that love out to the Universe. The Universe will match your vibration and you will attract more love into your life.

There are many ways you can raise your vibration. Sit outside and commune with nature. Drink more water. Eat foods that have a higher vibration. Live a healthy lifestyle. Think positive thoughts. Be happy. Be grateful. Be kind. Meditate. You get to choose what is best for you and your Highest Good.

Energy Centers

You have seven main chakras in your body. Chakras are energy centers that run through the center of your body, each correlating to a different area of your body. When these chakras are open and functioning properly, you are in a state of health, alignment and centeredness. When these energy centers are off balance, you experience a myriad of symptoms ranging from lack of self-esteem to closing your heart to love. Symptoms are specific to which chakra is unbalanced.

If you are feeling a bit off, your chakras may be out of balance or blocked. They can become blocked for many reasons. You may be going through trauma or addiction or maybe you have unresolved issues that you have not healed. All those feelings have an energy or vibration attached to them. When you can overcome them, you will raise your vibration.

How can you balance your chakras? Do some research and find out what you can about your chakras. There is a *ton* of information out there on the Internet and many good books as well. Once you figure out if any of your chakras are blocked or unbalanced you will be able to figure out what *you* specifically need to do to resolve that. Meditation and Reiki worked very well for me. Reiki is energy work. A Reiki practitioner lays their hands just above or on your body in different positions to assist in the flow of energy. It can help you release unhealed emotions, balance your chakras and help with relaxation among many other things. I started doing Reiki about twenty years ago. If you feel guided in that direction, I highly recommend it. If you are extremely tuned in to your body, you can feel your chakras opening up and expanding.

Removing Energy Blocks

You have been working on your issues for awhile now. How is that going for you? It is a tough workout, right? It is all a part of this wonderful awakening process. You must peel away the layers, one at a time, until you get to the core issues. Sometimes they masquerade themselves as something other than what they are. You may think you have healed an issue, then it pops up again as something else.

The thoughts you put out create energy. That energy then manifests itself into actions or things. If you are desiring a new job and you are putting out those thoughts of that new job, seeing yourself in the position you desire and seeing yourself with that big fat paycheck, you are doing all the right things, right? Well what if that job does not manifest? Were you doing it wrong all along? You can put out all the right thoughts and create all the right energy but, if you have hidden blocks within, you may well be pushing those very things away from you that you are trying to manifest.

I was having difficulty finding a job. I was doing all the right things to draw that job to me. I went on interview after interview after interview and *nothing*! During this time, I was doing a lot of inner work on myself. What I finally realized was that I was blocking all my good from coming to me. Even though I told the Universe *exactly* what I wanted it was never within my grasp. As I began to peel the layers away, I discovered something about myself that I would never have believed if someone else had told me, I did not feel I was worthy. I did not feel that I deserved to have that job. I realized that I did not love myself the way I thought or felt that I did.

As I had been doing my inner work, I was just *moving* the blocks around and never completely removing them. I never knew that was what I was doing. As issue after issue was revealed to me, I explored it, I healed it, and I moved past it. All along I did not realize that there was a very deep underlying issue, so deep and painful for me, that I masked it from myself. Was it my Higher Self trying to protect me? Was it my ego getting in the way? Maybe a little of both. I was determined to work through these blocks so that I could bring good, positive, and prosperous things into my life.

Although I was telling the Universe that I desired this awesome job, the energy that was exuding from my soul was telling the Universe that I did not deserve that really great job, or that I was not worthy of having it. Guess what? It did not come to me. Not until I dealt with the underlying core issue of my self-worth.

Meditation and really getting in touch with myself were the key ways I uncovered the blocks that were holding me back. Was it an easy process? Hell no! It was the *most* difficult work I have ever done. With great work comes great rewards. I love myself unconditionally in a way I never thought was possible. It has deepened the love I have for my children, family, and friends.

When all of this began coming to the surface and I realized how I felt about myself, I fell apart. I was crying uncontrollably, could not even stand up. I remember very clearly. It was so emotional. In order to have a breakthrough I had to have a breakdown. And break through did I ever! Once I learned to love and appreciate myself, my world changed. The energy I was now putting out there was pure, true, and authentically *me*!

I do not even know where my issues of unworthiness and lack of self-love came from. Perhaps they were remnants from broken relationships or even past life issues. The important thing is that I was able to address them and heal them.

While you are working on your issues, make sure you are getting to the very core of what they are. Make sure you are not just moving them around. This is hard work, but the payoff is unbelievable!

Manifesting

You can manifest whatever you want in your life. Once you have removed any blocks to abundance and balanced your chakras you are well on your way. When your energy or vibration matches the energy of what you want, you will manifest it. Have no fear or doubt about it. You must believe it with every fiber of your being. Have a vision for what it will look like in your life. See it. Feel it. Taste it. Live and breathe it. You must vibrate in the frequency of gratitude. Act like it has already been accomplished. You *will* manifest it in your life.

Remember that the energy you put out is matched by the Universe and sent back to you. Put out positive thoughts and loving vibrations. Once you take control of your thoughts and energy, you will learn that living in a vibration of gratitude will bring more things into your life for you to be grateful for.

Making the Connection

I feel very blessed to have learned the things I have learned as I travel along my path. Not only have I learned a lot about myself, but I have learned a lot about other people as well. My hope is that I can bring a little bit of Light into these areas and help you to open your mind and your heart to the Oneness of Humanity.

The Universe has quite a sense of humor. We search and search for our path, trying desperately to figure out where we belong. We finally get things figured out and start down that road that is meant only for us. The path is brightly lit for us to find our way.

We excitedly begin the journey only to find that the path is not a straight road. It winds and turns and has many obstructions along the way. Sometimes we come to a fork in the road and we have some heavy decisions to make. Sometimes it even takes us back to where we started. One thing is for sure, the journey is constant. It does not end. We move from one destination to another. The destination is not what is important. It is the journey and everything we learn along the way that is important.

We meet many people on our journey. Some will be purposefully put onto our path and sometimes we will purposefully be put onto others' paths. Everyone we meet, we meet for a reason. Everyone comes into our life for a reason. Sometimes we are the teacher and sometimes we are the student. We can learn something from everyone.

What I have learned about myself

All my past experiences and pains were caused by me in a sense, caused by my wrong way of thinking, of seeing things. When I changed my way of thinking, I realized that no one could harm me with their words or actions unless I allow them to.

We teach others how to treat us based on how we treat ourselves and what we feel we deserve. What we allow will continue.

Through a lot of emotional pain, I realized that I did not love myself in the same unconditional way that I thought I loved others. I have learned to love myself unconditionally. I have learned to fall in love with myself and to accept *everything* about me.

Everything I have experienced in my lifetime and everyone I have encountered in my lifetime have all been necessary to create the person I am and the person I will become.

The secret to being completely happy, fulfilled and passionate about life is to remember and live your purpose, your path, your journey. When you are traveling the road you are meant for, things will unfold smoothly and easily for you to advance in your journey.

The process or journey of awakening is continual, it is never over. It is not a destination you arrive at. It is a journey, a lifelong journey. A journey of learning, discovery and remembering. You will continue to grow and to peel away more layers, one by one.

Our intuition is the same thing as our Higher Self or Soul. It is our inner guidance system. It is always there to guide us along the way. It knows the truth even when we are not conscious of the truth. It has the answer to every question we will ever ask. We must learn how to be still and listen.

The choice is always ours. We can choose to be happy or we can choose to let our outer experiences bring us down and make us sad. We can choose to accept our path, or we can choose to ignore it. We can choose to love with all of our being or we can choose to withhold love from ourselves and others. We can choose to listen to our inner knowing or we can choose to ignore it. Every step of our journey we have a choice.

What I have learned about others

So many people live in a state of fear. Most of the time, this fear is completely unfounded. You fear things you *think* will happen. You fear things you do not understand. What most do not realize is that by putting those fears into thoughts, you create the energy of what you fear in the first place. Then, when you put out that vibration or energy, that is what the Universe sends back to you.

People are inherently good. You come from Love. You were created by Love. You *are* Love. People tend to fear the unknown. Learn about those things that you fear. Educate yourself and you will soon realize there is nothing to fear.

People do not realize you are a whole, complete being. You do not need anyone else to *complete* you.

You do not believe you are responsible for your own happiness. You look toward other people or things to make you happy. You place the burden of your happiness on something *out there*. That is not where happiness lies. It lies within each one of you. It is a choice you make each and every day. You do not need a reason to be happy. You are happy because you *choose* to be happy. Happiness is a state of being not a state of doing.

What I have learned about life

We are all sparks of the Divine. We are all unique beings of Divine Light and Love. We have all come to this Earth plane for a specific reason, a Divine Purpose. We determined our goals and purpose before we incarnated into this human form. We already know the answers and it is merely an act of remembering who we are and why we are here. We are all connected-all of humanity, nature, space. There is an invisible thread that connects all of life. You can be still and feel the connection. It is an amazing feeling to experience.

The Universe will repeatedly gift us with situations or challenges until we learn the lessons we need to learn from them.

Love is the highest vibration. It is the most important thing that exists. Love is who and what we are. Fear is the opposite of love. Love and fear cannot occupy the same space. We only fear something out of ignorance. When we educate ourselves about what we fear we shed some light and take the fear away. The only thing that is left is love.

Life goes on. It is a never-ending cycle of birth and rebirth. There is no such thing as death. Our soul simply leaves our body and travels on to another place to continue our never-ending journey.

The Journey Continues

I started this book with a little bit of background about me. I worked my way into the beginning of my Spiritual Awakening and what that looked like for me. Then I delved into some of the greatest lessons I have learned on my journey called life.

I touched on relationships, loss, change, purpose, and some other topics as well. Some of my words may greatly resonate with you, some may not. Maybe none will. That is okay.

Take what you need from my story as you are creating your own. No two people will have the exact same journey. There will be similarities as well as differences. There should be. Your journey is yours. This is mine.

Although this book is finally finished, *my story* is not. I continue to grow on every level. I continue to create change in my life. I continue to challenge myself to go above and beyond what my mind tells me I can do.

So, I challenge you
- ❖ To live your life outside of the box.
- ❖ To listen to your inner voice.
- ❖ To live every day to the fullest.
- ❖ Love, honor and respect yourself
- ❖ Smile because everybody needs one.

Thank you for taking the time to read my book. It is my intention that you took some information or comfort in something that you read. We all hear what we need to hear when we need to hear it.

Although this book was written entirely of *my* personal experiences, it is my intention that you can see yourself or some aspect of *your* life in these pages. Take comfort in knowing you are not alone in this life. We all have a story to tell, what is yours?

Everything is Possible!!!

Afterword

I would like to share some of my beliefs. I only focus on and give energy to that which I believe. I do not give energy to the things I do not like or believe. Only positive vibrations.

I believe in a Higher Power (God, The Universe, Spirit, whatever you choose to call it). I believe this Energy or Light is inside every one of us and every living thing. This Power is everywhere and experiences all.

I believe this Universal Force (God) is Love and Light.

I believe that although the physical body may cease to exist, we do not. I believe our Soul/Spirit lives on forever. Energy cannot be created or destroyed. It can only change form. That is what we do. We shed our physical skin like clothing and our Spirit chooses a new wardrobe.

I believe we all come to this Earth Plane with a Soul Purpose. I believe it is up to us to remember our reason for coming here, to remember what lessons we wanted to learn. To seek it out, claim it and manifest it.

I believe we map out our earthly experience for each life before we incarnate. We decide who we will be, what goals we wish to accomplish, we design our Soul Purpose and choose those who will assist us along our way. We are assigned Guides and Angels that are with us day to day, right by our sides.

I believe when we are born into this world, all prior knowledge is hidden from us in our subconscious. It is our task to uncover and remember all the knowledge we brought with us.

I believe that we can manifest everything we want for ourselves in our lives. If we can believe it, we will surely see it.

I believe we have Free Will and that we are responsible for our own actions.

I believe Hell is a state of being. It is created when you do not realize your true nature, or you turn away from your true self. You are living in a state of hell when you do not accept yourself for who you truly are.

I believe to be genuinely happy we must live in our authenticity and purpose. I believe this is the reason there are so many unhappy people in this world. They have not yet realized their Soul Purpose and are not in touch with who they really are. Once they do and they begin to align with their Purpose, their entire world will shift.

I believe that Jesus, Buddha, Saint Germain and others came here to be an example of what we could be. They were great Spiritual Teachers and Healers.

I believe Angels are always with us helping to guide

us along on our journey. They are always willing to assist us. All we must do is ask.

I believe the most important thing in this world is Love. It is the only thing that matters. It is the only thing that is real. Everything that is not of love is of fear. Fear is merely an illusion. We either see through the eyes of love or the eyes of fear.

These are *my* beliefs. They may or may not be yours as well. I will say that it really helped me to write them down and say them out loud. It was very empowering. These are not the same beliefs I had as a child. They have grown and expanded as I have.

After a lot of searching, I found what resonates with me...a direct, personal relationship with Source. Some define this as Spirituality. I do not feel the need to define my relationship with the Divine. It is what it is. Defining seems to limit what you are defining. It gives it definition and parameters that put limitations on it. My communication with the

Divine is limitless. It has no boundaries. I always choose to stay connected. I have built myself a wonderful *spiritual family* through work events and social media. I am surrounded by like-minded people. It truly is a gift and I am so incredibly grateful for the amazing people that have and continue to cross my path.

Everyone has their own Truth. It is what resonates with your Soul. Only *you* can figure that out. We each have our own set of beliefs and they will change as we grow and change. They are not right or wrong. You know what resonates with your Soul. Only you can say what is true for you. Stand in your beliefs and stand in your Power.

Please send me your personal stories about your spiritual journey. You can email them to MyStory@ruthsoltman.com or you can go to my website www.ruthsoltman.com and submit your story there. Some stories will be chosen for a future book.

For your comfort, you may remain anonymous so please send in your stories. I would love to read them. Much Love and Many Blessings to you all. Namaste.

About the Author

Ruth has had a lifelong passion for writing. She has an empathic understanding and deep compassion for the human condition, and it is reflected in her writing. She is dedicated to helping others wake up and realize the truth of who they are so they can live an authentic life.

Ruth is an Angelic Reiki Practitioner, Reiki Master and Angel Card Reader and lives in the Houston area.

Connect with Ruth
www.facebook.com/angelworkspublishing
www.facebook.com/iamruthsoltman
Twitter@ruthsoltman
Visit her at her website www.ruthsoltman.com

www.ingramcontent.com/pod-product-compliance
Lightning Source LLC
LaVergne TN
LVHW051522070426
835507LV00023B/3247